LET'S EXPLORE LIFE SCIENCE

Exploring Our IMPACT on the ENVIRONMENT

Ella Hawley

PowerKiDS
press.

New York

Published in 2013 by The Rosen Publishing Group, Inc.
29 East 21st Street, New York, NY 10010

First Edition

Editor: Jennifer Way
Book Design: Kate Laczynski

Photo Credits: Cover © www.iStockphoto.com/Dmitry Mordvintsev; cover (bulb, turbine), pp. 4–5, 6, 12, 14, 15 (left, right), 17, 18, 20–21, 21 (top), 22 Shutterstock.com; p. 7 George Doyle/Stockbyte/ Thinkstock; p. 8 © www.iStockphoto.com/Phototreat; p. 9 © www.iStockphoto.com/Jeremy Mayes; pp. 10–11 Sepavo/Shutterstock.com; p. 11 (main) Michael Dunning/Getty Images; p. 13 William F. Campbell/Time & Life Pictures/Getty Images; p. 16 © www.iStockphoto.com/PicsFive; p. 19 © www.iStockphoto.com/Lucyna Koch; p. 21 (bottom) Digital Vision/Thinkstock.

Library of Congress Cataloging-in-Publication Data

Hawley, Ella.
 Exploring our impact on the environment / by Ella Hawley. — 1st ed.
    p. cm. — (Let's explore life science)
 Includes index.
 ISBN 978-1-4488-6177-4 (library binding) — ISBN 978-1-4488-6308-2 (pbk.) —
ISBN 978-1-4488-6309-9 (6-pack)
 1. Nature—Effect of human beings on—Juvenile literature. I. Title.
GF75.H39 2013
 304.2—dc23

                                        2011027677

Manufactured in the United States of America

CPSIA Compliance Information: Batch #SW12PK: For Further Information contact Rosen Publishing, New York, New York at 1-800 237-9932

CONTENTS

What Is the Environment?

An **environment** is any place where plants and animals live. A backyard and pond are both environments.

The environment is important. If you change one part of an environment, other parts of that environment will change, too. For example, if you **pollute** the water in a pond environment, it changes how much algae grows. It could also hurt plants or animals that live nearby. The changes to that environment may change neighboring environments, too. How much you change an environment is called your impact on it. This book will teach you more about things that impact the environment.

The environment in this park includes tress, bushes, mosses, and a pond. Changes to one part of this environment can have an effect on other parts of it.

Dirty Air

People can be hard on the environment. We make a huge impact on the environment and do not do enough to protect it. One example of this is air pollution. We drive cars and make goods in factories. These things burn fuel, which pollutes the air.

Factories can give off air pollution in the forms of chemicals and soot.

6

Air pollution comes from all the dirty things we put into our air. These dirty things can be car **exhaust** or fumes from cleaners or paints we use. Many of the machines we use to help make our lives easier pollute the air. Air pollution causes health problems, such as **asthma**.

Asthma is a condition that causes breathing problems. For many people with asthma, air pollution makes the condition worse.

Water Pollution

Water pollution can happen when heavy rains wash waste from livestock or sewers into the water. **Pesticides** from farms pollute water, too. Polluted water can make the plants and animals that depend on it sick.

Oil spills also cause water pollution. An oil spill happens when a ship carrying oil has an accident. Many fish, marine mammals, and birds die from oil spills.

Oil Spill

Trash can pollute the water, too. Trash can come together to form large floating garbage patches. The largest one, called the Great Pacific Garbage Patch, is the size of Texas and has about 3.5 million tons (3.2 million t) of garbage in it!

GRAPHIC ORGANIZER: The Water Cycle

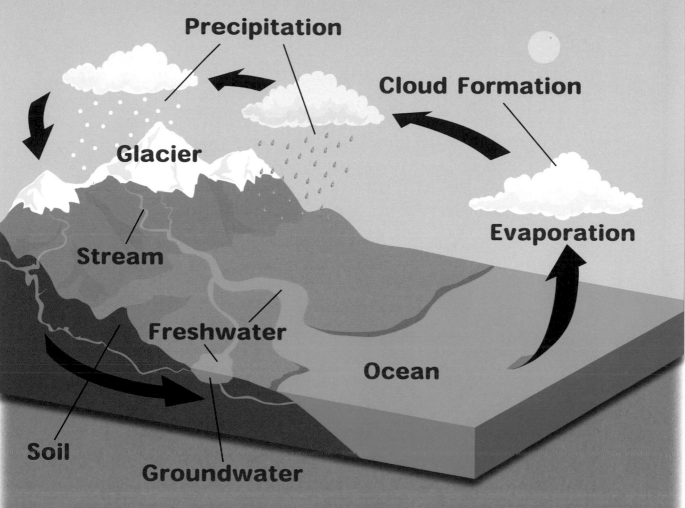

Precipitation

Cloud Formation

Glacier

Evaporation

Stream

Freshwater

Ocean

Soil

Groundwater

The water cycle is the constant movement of Earth's water. Water falls as precipitation. It is stored in glaciers, bodies of water, and groundwater. It evaporates into the air. Then it forms clouds, and the cycle starts again. Can you see how water pollution has a big effect on the environment?

A Crowded World

There are almost seven billion people on Earth, and that number is growing! All those people need food, medicine, homes, and more. It takes land to provide those things. As the human **population** grows, cities become overcrowded. When cities are too crowded, people spread out and take over more land.

Many of the world's cities are extremely crowded. The world's population is growing quickly. More than one million people are born every week!

People use a lot of other natural resources, too. Water is used for drinking, cleaning, and watering crops. Forests are cut down for lumber to build homes and furniture. We dig deep underground to get at oil, **minerals**, and coal. These things can all cause pollution and have a huge impact on the environment!

This photograph of Earth at night was made from hundreds of satellite pictures. The bright spots are cities lit up at night. This gives you an idea of how populated and urban much of the world is.

Habitat Loss

Many of the world's forests have been cut down for lumber or to build roads, homes, or businesses. The cutting down of forests is called deforestation, which is a cause of habitat loss.

When we cut down forests or clear land for homes, roads, or buildings, we are changing the environment. We are taking away **habitat** from plants and animals.

When plants and animals lose their homes, it is called habitat loss. Habitat loss is one of the biggest ways we hurt our environment. When animals lose their habitat, they must move and adapt to a new habitat or die. If a place becomes too populated, there is no longer space for animals to live or plants to grow. Birds cannot nest. Chipmunks have no place to dig burrows. No new birds or chipmunks are born in that habitat.

The northern spotted owl lives in the northwestern United States. It is one species that is threatened by habitat loss.

Going, Going, Gone!

The black rhinoceros lives in Africa. It is critically endangered, which means that its population is dropping very quickly.

Humans have caused the **extinction** of about 500 animal species since 1600. That means those types of animals no longer exist. There are around 5,000 **endangered** animal species today. That means that if we do not do something to help these animals, they will soon be gone, too. These numbers just include animals. There are many endangered plant species, too.

Today, people know that keeping the **biodiversity** of Earth safe is important. That is because plants, animals, and their environments are connected. Keeping these things balanced helps the environment.

The golden lion tamarin is an endangered monkey that lives in the rain forests of South America.

The giant panda is an endangered bear that lives in mountain forests in China.

Fossil Fuels

People use a lot of energy. We use energy to light, heat, and cool our homes and businesses. We use energy to make our cars run and to cook our food. Factories use energy to make all the things that people buy.

More than 85 percent of the energy used in the United States comes from coal, oil, and natural

These barrels of oil are an example of a nonrenewable resource. That means that once the world's oil supply has been drilled and used, there will be no more oil.

gas. These are all **fossil fuels**. Burning fossil fuels causes pollution, smog, and global climate change. The other problem with using fossil fuels is that they are not **renewable** sources of energy. We are using so much fossil fuel that we are in danger of running out.

Many things we use, including cars, burn fossil fuels. Fossil fuels will not last forever, and burning them causes pollution. People are working to invent ways to use less fossil fuel or to make better use of renewable resources, such as solar or wind power.

Climate Change

Burning fossil fuels puts greenhouse gases into the air. Greenhouse gases, such as carbon dioxide, trap heat inside the layer of gases around Earth, called the atmosphere. A certain amount of greenhouse gases helps Earth support life. Too many greenhouse gases can harm Earth.

The rise in greenhouse gases caused by burning fossil fuels is changing Earth's climate. Ice caps and

Melting ice in the Arctic causes habitat loss for polar bears. Melting ice also causes the sea level to rise, which can lead to flooding along coasts and affects the weather around the world.

glaciers are starting to melt. This hurts the animals, such as polar bears, that live in those icy habitats. Changes in climate affect the environment. If an area starts getting more rain, wetland areas could get larger. Other places may have longer droughts, or periods without rain.

Climate change is more than just warming temperatures. In some places, climate change could cause stronger storms or longer droughts and will affect people all over the world.

Reducing Our Impact

This house has solar panels on the roof. These panels soak up the Sun's energy so that it can provide electricity for the house. Solar energy is a renewable resource.

We now know how some of our actions have had a harmful impact on the environment. The good news is that scientists and the government are working hard to come up with new energy sources. Wind and solar power are two renewable energy sources. As **technology** gets better, these cleaner kinds of energy will be easier and cheaper to use.

Companies are also making products that use less energy or that do not pollute the air and water as much. There are better engines in cars. Paints can be made without matter that pollutes the air. Even with all these steps, there is still a long way to go!

Some new technologies are made to use less energy. This is called being energy efficient. A compact fluorescent lightbulb (right) uses less electricity than a regular lightbulb. It is energy efficient.

Wind power is another renewable resource. These machines, called turbines, collect the wind's energy and turn it into electricity. A group of turbines like this is called a wind farm.

How You Can Help

Luckily, you can help Earth by doing a few easy things. You can save energy by turning off lights when you leave a room. Closing the refrigerator door quickly helps keep cool air from leaving. You can save water by turning off the tap when you are brushing your teeth and by taking shorter showers.

Recycling helps save resources and cuts down on pollution. This helps reduce your impact on the environment.

Find out what can be recycled in your area, such as glass, metal, paper, and plastic. You can also find ways to reuse things. Try to buy fewer disposable things or things with wasteful packaging. Learning about our impact on the environment can give you even more ideas about how to be Earth friendly!

GLOSSARY

asthma (AZ-muh) A condition that makes it hard for a person to breathe.

biodiversity (by-oh-dih-VER-sih-tee) The number of different types of living things that are found in a certain place on Earth.

endangered (in-DAYN-jerd) In danger of no longer existing.

environment (en-VY-ern-ment) Everything that surrounds people and other living things and everything that makes it possible for them to live.

exhaust (ig-ZOST) Smoky air made by burning gas or other fuels.

extinction (ek-STINGK-shun) The state of no longer existing.

fossil fuels (FO-sul FYOOLZ) Fuels, such as coal, natural gas, or gasoline, that were made from plants that died millions of years ago.

habitat (HA-buh-tat) The kind of land where an animal or a plant naturally lives.

minerals (MIN-rulz) Natural matter that is not an animal, a plant, or another living thing.

pesticides (PES-tuh-sydz) Poisons used to kill pests.

pollute (puh-LOOT) To poison with harmful matter.

population (pop-yoo-LAY-shun) A group of animals or people living in the same place.

renewable (ree-NOO-uh-bul) Able to be replaced once it is used up.

technology (tek-NAH-luh-jee) The way that people do something using tools and the tools that they use.

WEB SITES

Due to the changing nature of Internet links, PowerKids
Press has developed an online list of Web sites related
to the subject of this book. This site is updated regularly.
Please use this link to access the list:
www.powerkidslinks.com/lels/impact/